The Tale of Genevieve
A DOLPHIN'S LULLABY
To The Sea

WRITTEN BY KRISTEN HALVERSON

ILLUSTRATED BY WINDHA SUKMANINDYA

Cover and Interior Illustrations by Windha Sukmanindya

Second Edition (Hardcover)

Published by Kristen Halverson

14104 225th Street

Elkader, Iowa

www.kristenhalverson.com

ISBN 978-1-64370-917-8

This book is a work of fiction. Places, events, and situations in this book are purely fictional and any resemblance to actual persons living, or dead, is coincidental.

To my grandmother,
Pearl, who loved everything about the sea.

Deep within the blue sea, there lived a musical dolphin named Genevieve.

Genevieve loved to swirl and twirl through rolling waves. She spent her days splashing through peach, coral caves.

Her grandmother, Pearl taught Genevieve how to whistle best. Genevieve's peaceful sound helped her sea friends rest.

Genevieve made a magical,
bedtime whistle every night.
It lit up the sea like a beautiful,
rainbow night light.

Playful and colorful seahorses
would sway and neigh.

Tiny, green sea turtles
were happy; it was the
end of the day.

Bright, red lobsters were her biggest sea fans. They laid their heads on soft, pink clams.

Graceful starfish floated like a glowing kite. It was an incredible sight!

The heavenly melody helped the clever octopus curl in a ball like a tiny doll.

The kind, yellow butterfly fish knew her song was a nighttime call. It made their eyes very small.

The curious crab rested on
a silver sand dollar.
The whale whispered
a comforting holler.

Genevieve's whistle echoed through the sea. It made the whole ocean family feel free. The magic of her whistle hummed, "You can become anything you want to be!"

As the ocean family rested for the night. Genevieve's enchanting whistle made her friends' peaceful dreams take flight.

The End

www.ingramcontent.com/pod-product-compliance
Lightning Source LLC
Chambersburg PA
CBHW042029090426
42811CB00016B/1790